From Promise to Delivery:
Conceiving and Delivering the Promises of God

By

LaToya Stevens

From Promise to Delivery:
Conceiving and Delivering the Promises of God

Copyright by CECO Publishing

All Rights Reserved. No part of this book can be reproduced or transmitted in any form without written permission from the author.

For Booking & Contact Information:
cecopublishing@gmail.com

All scripture references are from the King James Version of the Holy Bible, unless otherwise noted.

All Greek and Hebrew translations and definitions are from The Strong's Concordance unless otherwise noted.

Brown-Driver-Briggs Hebrew and English Lexicon, Hedrickson Publishers ©1996.

Thayer's Greek-English Lexicon of the New Testament, Hendrickson Publishers © 1996.

Cover design by LaToya Stevens

ISBN: 978-0-9836336-0-0

CECO Publishing

What People Are Saying About

From Promise to Delivery: Conceiving and Delivering the Promises of God

"There are a lot of people of the ecclesiastical establishment that have with a precise eloquent dissertation, perfected the Logos; but very few have mastered including the RHEMA { the what God is saying now} with Logos as Solid Foundation. I confess after reading "From Promise to Delivery", it's mandated for this season and time and surely is on time from a true Vessel of God Elder LaToya Stevens. As stated in her book that the only way to know God is through his Word. I throw that same word out and that you will come to know the heart of this Great Fine TUNED Elder that just so happens to be a preacher through the Life changing faith facts she gives in this book. It will help you handle what you carry so you can make it to Delivery Status. Grab you a Copy.....Shalom & Amen"

Apostle Michael Lampkin,
Fresh Anointing Prosperity Ministries
St Louis, Missouri

"This book is profoundly revelatory! I found myself wanting to preach at the fourth chapter! Preachers be forewarned; this book will make the preacher preach and make the doubter become a believer! No matter your level or position in the Kingdom, or life in general, we are all wanting and waiting on something greater; the message in this writing helps the reader to clearly navigate towards the manifestation of that greater thing. This book is a must read, must have, and a guaranteed blessing to the Body of Christ!"

Overseer LaMont Walker
International Overseer of Music
Christians Equipping Christians for Outreach Fellowship
Columbia, Missouri

"Elder Stevens delves into the pieces that so many Christians overlook when living the promises of God. This book intellectually and plainly guides the reader from conception to the birth of what God has truly promised them!"

Pastor Nikesha Luther
New Hope Christian Center
Boonville, Missouri

Dedication

To my Lord, and Savior Jesus Christ, I am well aware that without you I am, and can do nothing. I'm amazed and humbled that you called me, and I will endeavor to live worthy of Your call.

To my husband, David you know you are more important to me than I can put into words. You encouraged me when I wanted to quit, and let me have my moment and come back around. Thank you for not allowing me to settle, I love you!

To my boys, David, Marcus, Matthew, and Nathaniel, thank you for sharing me with ministry and school. You guys are the best sons ever. Know that God has GREATNESS in store for each of you, and I love you.

Table of Contents

Prologue   13

Foreword
Bishop Dr. Russell L. Freeman   15

Chapter 1
Recognizing Your Season   17

Chapter 2
Conceiving the Promise   24

Chapter 3
What's the Condition of Your Spiritual Womb?   28

Chapter 4
Faith as Your Foundation   34

Chapter 5
The Nature of the Promise   39

Chapter 6
God's Role in the Promise   46

Chapter 7
The Progression of the Promise   54

Chapter 8
Delivering the Promise   66

Epilogue
When the Promise Transforms
Bishop H.D. Ware, Jr.   73

Appendix   81

Sermon Transcript
"You Want It, but Can You Carry It?"   83

About the Author   95

PROLOGUE

As we walk through life we make promises, promises to ourselves and to others. We believe that we can deliver on them *(sometimes)* and sometimes we KNOW that we cannot. Nevertheless we promise anyway. It is that tug of war between the lies we tell ourselves and the lies we tell each other that make it nearly impossible for us to believe the promises God makes to us.

The nature of a promise of God has been lost on a culture that does not believe anything anyone says and has learned to always look for an angle. Well, I want you to know that with God there is no angle other than your best interests and well being.

Through this book I will endeavor to address some critical areas in the lives of believers. Some problem areas prohibit the conception of the promises given to us by God. While others lead to the loss of the promise. My goal is to explain through the Word of God how we progress from receiving the promise to our ability to carry and deliver it.

His in Service,

Elder T. Stevens

FORWARD

Elder Stevens has received a divine message concerning the promises of God. Insight is given concerning how the understanding of God's promises will affect the church and the saints of God from every walk of life.

The church has need of understanding God's Promises for the restoration pertaining to God's people or all believers in the Word of God. Conceiving and delivering God's promises are essential throughout the Word of God. The New Testament Church must be encouraged and be aware to do all possible to bring completion to what God is building through us, the church.

Every saint of God will gain much encouragement through the study of this book. It is truly an inspiration for truth and revelation from the heart and mind of God. I am in agreement with this book. As a major promoter of individual and church growth, I can commend this book as being a positive contribution to what God is doing within His church. We thank Elder T Stevens for this wonderful opportunity to be encouraged and mindful as to what God is doing in our lives.

Dr. Russell Larry Freeman
Bishop
United Community Cathedral Church
Columbia, Missouri, USA

CHAPTER 1

Recognizing Your Season

"To every thing there is a season, and a time to every purpose under the heaven:"
Ecclesiastes 3:1

Throughout my experience on this earth I have learned that we live in a never ending cycle of seasons. However, we often times never see the ending of one season and the beginning of another. Seasons change and most of the time we miss it! Or, we believe that simply because our status or situation has changed, that means our season has changed as well. However, they do not always work together like that. There are times when your status or situation can change yet you remain in the same season you were in prior to that change.

Seasons are often preached and taught about in the church, after all it is in the book of Ecclesiastes 3:1 that we learn, "To every *thing there is* a season, and a time to every purpose under the heaven:"(King James Version). This scripture puts a couple of principles into play. Number 1: everything has a season. Number 2: everything has a time. Did you see that? There is *first* a season but within it lies a specific time.

There are times in life when our season will change. It is helpful to first be able to recognize when a change of season is occurring. In the natural it is the axis of the earth that determines what season you are in. During the winter months you get less sunlight producing colder days. However, during the summer months you receive more sunlight producing warmer days.

This can parallel with believers', whatever you are most inclined to, whatever is reaching you most will determine your growth? Is it self? Or is it the Son? If it's the latter then you are in an optimal position for growth and the steady progression of seasons. Ultimately, God determines when a season ends and begins. He determines this based off of the growth and development of our relationship with Him.

While what follows next is not intended to be a complete guide to recognize what season you are in, it is a nice guide to show you what I have recognized in the arena of spiritual seasons.

Spring

When spring arrives we are so happy for the simple fact that's it's not winter and we get to get out and do more! It's the same spiritually. When our winter months have finally ended we are excited! You can see some areas in your life where have grown since winter, and although it's small growth, hey it's growth right! You can also see what God planted and you are making sure it gets what it needs. So that in time, it produces fruit.

Spring is always a nice contrast to winter, but we tend to forget that spring has some things we should watch for. We are so ready to grow and move in the Lord, that *we* begin to move. We have spent so much time with Him it's almost like the atmosphere around us becomes thick with His presence. There's nothing wrong with that, but what happens when two different atmosphere collide in the natural? Tornados can occur and have the ability to tear up everything in their path. So be sure that you are mindful of your condition and don't be in such a hurry that you set yourself up for a potential disaster, by allowing yourself to come into contact with things that are contrary to God. He will never mix with mess! In fact, He will uproot everything that is not like Him!

Summer

In the summer everything is great! It is the time when you are able to concretely see the fruit that has been produced in your life. The minor growth you saw during the spring has had more time to grow. It may not be time for harvest yet, but it's obvious that it's there. Who doesn't like to see, the fruits of their labor? During the summer we thrive and we grow!

We are consistent in our service to God and we can hear very clearly. We may even have more ministry opportunities available and we accept them at the leading of the Spirit. During summer the days are also the longest they will be, and we are eager to work. We have the John 9:4 work mentality during the summer, "I must work the works of him that sent me, while it is day: the night cometh, when no man can work".

However, like spring there are thing to look out for. During the summer spiritually you will begin to see weeds trying to sprout up and grow with you. I'm sure you've seen it in the natural. You have a flower bed and you are excited when everything is blooming, it looks great (spring). Then you wait a couple months and you see all these weeds starting to spring up (summer). At first you are vigilant, and you pull the weeds you see right away. Then after a while you don't really notice until they're huge and what could have been pulled up with relative ease now take much more time and effort.

Be mindful of who/what is making deposits in your life or you could look up and need a tow truck to pull them out. Be vigilant! Although it's summer you have to protect the promise.

Fall

All though summer is great, we still get to the point where we are ready for fall, which is a nice break from the work of summer. Fall is the season of spiritual harvest. It is the time when all the fruit we watched grow during the summer months has finally matured. During the fall however the night starts to get longer and you see the inevitable countdown to winter.

The first sign is that your environment begins to change. The days start to get shorter and this is the time that you should be more mindful of the kind of work you are doing to optimize your growth. As a result your relationships start to change. Some relationships you have had forever begin to shift and some just slowly die and fall off like the leaves. When you see those relationships changing and others ending don't mourn them. It is simply a necessary step and they have already served their purpose in your life.

Winter

Spiritually the winter months are the harshest months. It is during this time that there is no growth to speak of and everything that is taking place in your life is under the surface. There are no bright green leaves, the sun seems like it will never come out and it is cold! Ministry may be slow and you come to realize it's just you and God and even He seems distant right now. During the winter you are pressed by your environment into developing a deeper relationship with the Lord. So while, on the surface winter seems like a waste of time, it is far from it. We survive the winter months because of what we stored in the spring and summer.

My prayer is that we all recognize when we are in the 'summer' months of our walk. It is in those months that we are storing up what we will need in order to live during the coming winter months. We would all like to stay in the spring when we are blossoming or the summer when we are thriving and growing, but fall and winter will inevitably cycle around and it is imperative to have something to sustain you during those months.

If we are not careful our faith will waver and instead of standing on what God promised, we will write it off, and just ask God to do 'a new thing'. 'What's the harm in that?', you may be asking yourself. Why would God give you something else, if you do not believe He can give you what He has already promised?

God gives us promises and it tends to be during the fall and winter that we decide to make things happen. We have all done it *at least* once. God makes us a promise and it takes too long to manifest and we begin to take steps to make it happen ourselves. Be mindful that just like in the natural, spiritually things can be produced out of season but it will always come at a much higher cost!

CHAPTER 2

Conceiving the Promise

"Through faith also Sarah herself received strength to conceive seed, and was delivered of a child when she was past age because she judged him faithful who had promised".
Hebrews 11:11

Conception in the natural is the moment you become pregnant. What does that mean spiritually? How do we conceive the promises of God? Hebrews 11:11 gives the answer: "Through faith". Faith is the crux of conception. In Hebrews 11:6, we learn that without faith it is impossible to please God. We also learn that faith is the substance of things hoped for, the evidence of things not seen (Hebrews 11:1).

Paul tells us in Romans 10:17 that, "faith comes by hearing and hearing by the Word of God". How do you hear? You listen! Do you listen to just anyone? I don't. I listen more to people I have a relationship with. So in order to have faith, you have to have a relationship with God. You have to talk to him, but most importantly He has to talk to you. You have to get to know Him through His Word.

Through that, intimacy develops. In the natural in order to get pregnant there has to be a level of intimacy. The same applies with God; there has to be spiritual intimacy, a level that goes beyond the fickle nature of man. The intimacy I'm talking about is God communing with your spirit. However, that level of intimacy requires that you be in the Spirit consistently enough for God to be able to make a deposit when He sees fit. The problem with believers today is *not* that we lack consistency, but that we are consistently inconsistent.

Don't get conceiving confused with understanding. The truth is when God is ready to move, He does, whether you understand it or not. Your job is not to understand, but to have faith that He is able to do what He has promised.

Scripture is full of those who received the promises of God and had those promises fulfilled. However, there were also those in scripture who were made a promise, yet did not receive it. The children of Israel were promised something, but their lack of faith prohibited some of them from actually entering the promise. Then Moses got to see the promise, but never got to possess it.

The Importance of Strength

In Hebrews 11:11 we see that Sarah needed "strength". She never had the strength necessary for conception, because she didn't have faith. In that verse strength goes back to the Greek word *dunamis* which literally translates to the *force, miraculous power, ability.*

Have you ever found yourself in Sarah's position; asking God for things, telling Him the desires of your heart and yet it never seems to come to pass? Or, God has made you a promise and it just does not seem like it will ever come to pass? My question to you is: Do you have the ability to conceive what God has for you? Do you have faith? More importantly is the environment in your life conducive with intimacy with God?

You may be asking yourself, "How am I supposed to be intimate with God?" Easily, spend time with Him. Get to know Him through His Word. The more time you spend with Him the deeper your relationship will be with Him. The level of trust grows. The relationship is no longer one sided, but it is reciprocal. You move beyond simply seeking God when *you* need something, because you now recognize that it is not all about you. The relationship is no longer about your needs or convenience but it shifts to what God desires of you, whether it's convenient or not.

As your relationship develops God will begin to speak to your destiny. He will begin to tell you some things that He has in store for you in the future. In other words, He makes you promises! It is important to understand that simply because He made you a promise this does not mean that there has been conception. Conception depends on two things: 1) your belief and 2) your actions lining up with your belief. These are both manifestations of your faith!

Without faith it is impossible to please God because you prohibit His ability to move in the earth. In order to conceive you must have faith. You have to develop a relationship with God based on love and seek after Him. So what happens when you have done all of that and you still do not see any signs of the promise manifesting in your life? You have to ask yourself a question! What is it on the inside of me that will contaminate the seed of God's promise?

CHAPTER 3

What's the Condition of Your Spiritual Womb?

"And Sarai said unto Abram, Behold now, the LORD hath restrained me from bearing:"
Genesis 16:2a

So what happens when you have spent the time with God and you receive the deposit, but conception still doesn't occur? What causes us to kill what God gives us before we ever get to see it manifest? Let me ask you the way He asked me! "What is it on the inside of you that is so nasty that it will contaminate what I put on the inside of you? Is your womb at best hostile or are you barren?"

Those are tough but necessary questions. The womb is the part of you that secures what has been deposited in you by God until such a time as it is ready to be manifest in the natural. The timeline for spiritual pregnancy is entirely dependent upon your spiritual maturity, the condition of your womb and the amount of time God deems necessary for you to change and grow and for the promise to grow and develop.

Let's keep a of couple things in mind. Simply because you are pregnant does not mean that you are mature enough to handle the manifestation of the full promise. In fact it means something totally different. It means that right now you are in the optimal position to nurture the seed so that it can grow. Neither the seed nor you are ready for the full manifestation. Both require growth and development. The promise, so it can live in the natural and you to ensure you are ready mentally, physically, and spiritually to take care of it.

In the natural when you are pregnant it starts off small. You don't even know you are pregnant at first and no one else does either. However, with enough time it is evident to you that you are pregnant and it also becomes evident to others.

Are You Barren?

In Genesis 16:2a Sarai tells her husband that she cannot have kids. The interesting part is that she knows why she can't have kids. She states, "the LORD hath restrained me from bearing:" That word *restrained* comes from the Hebrew word `atsar which means to close up to shut up. In that scripture we see that Sarai knows she can't have children and she also knows why she can't have kids, but she still wants them. I know I have had times when I knew God was preventing something from happening and

I went out of my way to make it happen (maybe that's just me though)!

Sarai knew that God closed her womb. Let's face it, in the natural people had probably already told her she was barren and she believed she was too. After all, God closed her womb remember! That is what happens when you are barren spiritually. God closes your womb. It doesn't matter how much your pastor lays hands on you and prays for you. It doesn't matter because the LORD has closed your womb and *only He can open it*. The catch is there are things we have to get right in our relationship in order for conception to be a possibility.

There are inherent dangers with producing things when God is not part of the equation. And, if you keep reading you will see Sarai figured she could manage to get what she wanted without ever consulting God. Genesis 16:2b reads, "I pray thee, go in unto my maid; it may be that I may obtain children by her. And Abram hearkened to the voice of Sarai".

"Go in, unto my maid", in desperation she opened herself up for drama that God never intended. We do the same thing, we open ourselves up to trials He never designed for us. "It *may be* that I *may* obtain children by her" (emphasis added). It "may" be. Sarai now is rolling the dice and hoping that her maid stays in line and does what was then the custom of the day.

You see, back then, custom said if you could not have children your maid could have them and turn the child over to the master and their wife for them to raise as their own. However, if you are familiar with this account you know that is not what happened. Abraham did not just lay with her. Nope! He married her. Now, she was on the same playing field as Sarai. That was not in Sarai's plan; she just wanted a child. But now her husband has another wife (Hagar), and she decided she wants to keep her son. Sarah's impulsive action has lead her to a 14 year lesson!

This is what our plans look like! We think we have covered all the bases only to learn out we have no control over other people. We end up like Sarai, dealing with the consequences of man-made decisions instead of living in the abundance of divine provision. That is why Sarai was barren! Her lack of faith, and because she lacked faith she went about doing things her own way.

Is Your Womb Hostile?

Let's start with the good news! The problem with most believers in the Body of Christ is *not* that we are barren! Whew! That means that we have the ability to conceive what God has promised us. Now, to the not so good news, most of us have hostile wombs.

You may be wondering what a hostile womb is. A hostile womb is one in which your womb creates an environment that kills the seed before conception can occur. Or, you conceive but the environment in your womb is hostile and it aborts the seed on its own.

Here we have two scenarios. One in which your womb prevents conception. In the other scenario, conception occurs, but because your womb doesn't recognize it, it aborts the pregnancy. Your body views the deposit as foreign and turns on it.

Let's put this in perspective. You have spent time with God and developed that intimacy with Him through relationship; but when He tells you there is a work to be done you say, "Who me? You must have me confused with someone else. I can't do that". Then he sends someone to confirm it and you don't receive it. Newsflash! Your womb is hostile and you have just killed what God deposited before you had the opportunity to conceive.

Another perspective is God tells you there is a work for you to do and you receive it. He sends someone that confirms what He told you and it resonates with your spirit and you conceive, but then you begin to doubt and lose faith. Now your womb is no longer compatible with the things of God and has officially become hostile. Eventually you stop working toward what God gave you and the vision dies, your womb is also hostile.

It is imperative as Christians that we actually *believe* what God tells us. There is no requirement that you understand how, or that you even agree. He only asks that you trust Him; because when you don't, it is an insult to Him. He spends time with you and develops a relationship with you and then deposits His vision in you and you don't trust Him? What kind of relationship is that?

Your spiritual womb can be contaminated by your flesh. As we discussed in the previous chapter faith is the crux of both conception and successful delivery of the things of God. We know faith is critical, but let's discuss the importance of faith as our foundation.

CHAPTER 4

Faith as Your Foundation

"Now faith is the substance of things hoped for, the evidence of things not seen".
Hebrews 11:1

Faith by biblical definition is: "the substance of things hoped for, the evidence of things not seen" (Hebrews 11:1). We all know this scripture!!! We can quote it when asked, "What is the biblical definition of faith?" However, I have another question: What in the world does that mean exactly? Sure we know what it says, but do we know what it means? How is faith both *substance* and *evidence*? When we have a full understanding of this scripture we will have a clear view as to why faith is so vital in the process of conceiving, carrying, and birthing the promises of God.

Faith as Substance

Let's start with getting an understanding of what substance is. Substance in that scripture goes back to the Greek word *hupostasis*. This word is defined in the Thayer Greek Dictionary in part as, "thing put under, substructure, foundation". So, faith is the foundation of things hoped for!

As you may know, the foundation is the most important part of the house. If you think about it, the foundation supports the entire weight of the house and anything that will be put inside of it. So if the foundation is not solid it can cause the whole house to collapse.

The same is true with our faith. Our faith or conviction of a thing is the foundation of our hope. As previously stated Hebrews 11, says "faith is the substance of things hoped for" What is hope? Your hope is the vision or promise of God. Where a lot of believers get confused is in thinking that your hope/vision or promise is the actual moment of conception. Simply having a vision does not make you pregnant. It is your hope for the future, based on the promise of God.

Faith gives you a foundation to hold the weight associated with your promise. The promises of God all come with a measure of weight. Most of the weight comes from the realization that He trusts you with His vision! The weight is in understanding the gravity of the promise and your responsibility to God through it.

Faith as Evidence

Faith is also described as, "the evidence of things not seen". In Hebrews 11:1 "evidence" is translated back to the Greek word *elegchos*. Which simply put is your conviction. Your evidence is your belief. Do you see this; it is a huge circle. Your faith is what shifts the promise from hope to reality.

Evidence is what a belief is based on. When there is a trial there is evidence presented to a jury. The evidence is what shapes the thoughts and perception of the jury. In much the same way our faith is what shapes our thoughts and perception of what God has promised, although we may not see it.

When faith is used correctly, it allows you to hold up the weight of what God promised. It allows you to withstand the attacks of the enemy because it shapes how you view and think about your situation and your promise.

Conception can only occur when you receive the vision God has for you through faith. However, there is a little more than that. We discussed in Chapter 2 the importance of intimacy and relationship with God. It is not until you actually believe what God as promised you and your actions line up with your beliefs that you move beyond having a hope or vision for the future, to pulling into today through conception.

God is waiting on many of us to have faith in what He says. He is also waiting on others to believe Him more than they believe their situations or circumstances. Hebrews 11:11 states, "Through faith also Sara herself received strength to conceive seed…" The word, conceive means foundation. In Chapter 2 we talked about her receiving *dunamis,* or power, and ability to conceive. So, through faith Sarah received the ability and capacity, by the power of God, to have a foundation so she could conceive the seed that God promised her.

That is where so many of us are today! We are waiting on an endowment of power to conceive and deliver what God has for us. If you keep reading Hebrews 11:11 you will see when she got her endowment, she received only when, "...she judged him faithful who had promised".

We have a tendency to get sidetracked by issues that are not relevant to what God has promised us. We look at everything except the important thing which is God. Sarah didn't conceive because just anyone told her she would conceive. She did because God told her she would conceive. Let's take a look at that passage of scripture so we can get some of the back story.

Faith to Receive the Promise

Sarah's lack of a foundation is what kept her barren. Her lack of faith literally prevented God from moving in her life. In Genesis 18, Abraham is told by the Angel of the Lord that He will return and Sarah will have a son "according to the time of life" (Genesis 18:10). At this point she is 89 years old and of course she finds the idea hilarious! So much so, that she literally laughs to herself when she hears this.

What happens next is where we are focusing. The Angel of the Lord says in verse 14, "Is anything too hard for the LORD? At the time appointed I will return unto thee, according to the time of life, and Sarah shall have a son". You may be wondering, "What is the time of life?' In that scripture life means in part, strong. So the appointed time can be 2011, while the time of life is the specific date when you are strong enough to carry the promise in 2011.

When you have and are operating in faith you recognize that there is nothing too hard for the LORD. That God is capable of doing *exactly* what He said He would do. You realize that faith is the foundation of your promise, it is the proof of the promise you don't see, and it shapes your thoughts and perception of it! You don't have a foundation just to have one; it is there to be built on! Let's strengthen our foundation so it can withstand the weight of God's vision.

CHAPTER 5

The Nature of the Promise

"Now the LORD had said unto Abram, Get thee out of thy country, and from thy kindred, and from thy father's house, unto a land that I will shew thee:"
Genesis 12:1

Often times we treat a promise that God makes us the same as we treat a promise made to us by man. We have lost the ability to understand to fullness of a promise of God. It is that lack of understanding that prevents so many of us from conceiving and carrying it. We cannot carry the promise if we do not recognize it. What is the nature of the promise? Simply defined its nature is how it can be recognized, its characteristics. Looking again at Sarah and Abraham we begin to see a couple of characteristics to look for.

Genesis 12:1 starts off quite profoundly! "Now the LORD had said unto Abram". This shows us that although there is nothing in the text that states that Abraham and the LORD had any previous conversations there was something on the inside of Abraham that bore witness that it was the LORD. He recognized the voice and knew who was speaking to him. What follows next gives a few indicators that it was a promise of God.

Some Assembly Required

We have all seen that statement. You buy something from the store and the only way to see the finished product is to take action ourselves. The same is true with our spiritual promises. God requires us as He required Abram to take action, in order to see the promise. Often times we think about the promises of God from the perspective that it is simply something we get to receive without having to put any work in for it. That simply is not the case. God's promises always require action on our part, even if the only action necessary is faith.

Abram had to leave the country he was living in, his family, and everything attached to his father. Here is the biggest thing from my perspective. He had to leave everything he was familiar with for a destination that would only be revealed to him after he left, when God was ready!

In return for Abram's obedience the Lord promised him He would make him a great nation. God also told Abram He would bless him, make his name great, and that he would be a blessing. What is interesting is that, as far as, God was concerned making Abraham a 'great nation' was *not* the blessing, neither was making his name great. Those were by products of God blessing him. Another by-product that is greatly overlooked is that God designed for Abraham to be a blessing to others. God does not bless you, just for you! So, if the 'promise' of God to you only involves you, you *may* want to question if He is the one making the promise.

God went on to tell Abram that not only did his obedience have an effect on him, but it would impact others as well. God said I will bless those that bless you and curse those that curse you. Also, that all the families of the earth would be blessed. What we do with what God's promises us effects others, but only if we are obedient.

Get in Position for His Presence

Genesis 12:4 starts with 10 of the most important words in Abraham's life! "So Abram departed, as the Lord had spoken unto him;". We have got to learn how to leave when God tells us to. Our promise hinges on our obedience, which is tied to our faith. We obey because we believe. We believe because we have faith in God. Our faith should not hinge on the details God reveals to us. With time the promise got more detailed. However, the first test of faith for Abraham was if he would leave everything he was familiar with; without knowing where he was going. To inherit a promise that he could not see.

When the promise is presented to Abram initially it is spoken. This required an assurance on the part of Abram of who he was talking to. After he actually left and began on his journey to pursue the promise, then the Lord *appeared* to him. Have you ever wondered, "why God hasn't shown up for me?" "Why did He promise me this and He is nowhere to be found?" Could it be that you haven't done what is required of you, in order for him to show up? God invests in us, when He deposits His vision. Are you producing dividends? If you aren't even in the position to move when He tells you, then you aren't in position for His presence.

When the Lord appeared to Abram he told him, "Unto thy seed will I give this land" (Genesis 12:7). Do you see that? God had no reason to appear if Abram had not left and been where he needed to be to be able to see what was just spoken. It shifted from a promise to a reality with his obedience. What was Abram's first response? He built an altar to the Lord and worshipped. This is crucial because I believe it is why he was chosen by God in the first place.

John 4 says that God is seeking true worshippers that will worship Him "in spirit and in truth". Why is that important? Notice the scripture does not say that God seeks worship. Worship is the act. God seeks worshippers, people who know and respond to His presence. When you know, who He is then you can get in position to hear from Him.

After leaving a place of worship Abram finds himself between Beth'-el and Hai. What is the significance? Beth'-el translates to 'the house of God' and Hai translates to "heap of ruins". Have you ever experienced a time of worship with the Lord? A time of sincere gratitude and before you know it you find yourself between the house of God and a heap of ruins? My question to you is, 'what is your response?' Is it to complain to God and anyone else who will listen about how much it sucks to be where you are? Or are you like Abram? Have you come to a place that regardless of where you are and what you are surrounded by you can build an altar unto the Lord and call upon His name? Abram cried out to God; then he picked himself up and kept going.

Famine in the Land

Abram get's to the land God promised only to find out that there was a famine. In order to escape the famine he goes to Egypt. When he gets there, he lies about who his wife is, saying she is his sister. Why is this important? It shows that God can and still does use whoever He wants! He does not require perfection on our part., but there has to be obedience and a willingness to repent.

Pharaoh takes Sarai as his wife and God plagues Pharaoh's house. Pharaoh gives Sarai back to Abram and sends them away with everything they possessed. What is the significance? We can end up in messes and because our purpose is vital to the Kingdom, God *can* cover us. Please don't take this as the green light to create messes and expect God to clean them up. You can mess around and frustrate His grace.

As soon as Abram is delivered from the mess he created in Egypt his first stop is the last place he experienced God. He went back to the altar he built and once again called on the name of the Lord. When I first read that I had to ask myself, would that be my response? When he is done he finds that the people who tend to his cattle are fighting with his nephew Lot's people over the land, because there was not enough to sustain them both.

Abraham asks Lot to separate himself and lets him decide where he will live. Only after Abraham and Lot were separate did the Lord appear to him again. Sometimes, God will allow people to start out on the journey with us, but they are not meant to be with us for the duration. Other times, we bring people with us God never intended to make the journey. Eventually, there will come a time of separation.

We often act like we need God to tell us it's time to end something. When someone is spiritually draining and you don't have enough for yourself, *why* does God need to tell you to separate yourself? Take note from Abraham. Lot was good company I'm sure, but when it was causing unnecessary drama Abraham separated himself to keep the peace. Little did he know the Lord would appear to him and let him know that all the land he could see would belong to him and his seed for ever.

God's promise will require that we take ownership of what He has for us. He gave Abram the land, but how much he got was dependent upon how far he could see and how far he willing to walk to secure his possession of it. How far can you see and are you willing to do the work to possess it?

How do we recognize the promise of God?

- It will always involve us being a blessing to someone else.
- It will require faith.
- It requires vision *and* work.

CHAPTER 6

God's Role in the Promise

"For when God made promise to Abraham, because he could swear by no greater, he sware by himself,"
Hebrews 6:13

When you see the chapter title you may be thinking, 'What kind of title is that? I know God's role!' I would encourage you to continue reading as we walk through some things.

Abraham was a man of faith. He was the first person this was attributed to in the Bible; his faith was counted to him as righteousness. Keep in mind the importance of that comment. We are considered righteous now only because of the blood of Christ. It is His blood that brings us in to right standing with God. Abraham did not have the luxury of the blood of Christ. His *faith* was counted to him as righteousness. We similarly are justified by our faith, but through faith in Christ.

Now, that we see one link between Abraham's promise and ours let's look at another. God is *the* most important link. Now, we all know that God is the Promiser. What does that mean to us, as believers?

The Promiser/Promisee Relationship

In any transaction there is a promiser and a promisee. The promiser is responsible for ensuring the promisee gets whatever was promised. However, this happens only after certain stipulations are met. In the natural if you are promised something there is a contractual obligation by the promiser to fulfill the promise. If that is the case in the natural, it stands to reason that the same concept applies spiritually.

In Genesis 15, God expands His role from that of a promise giver to include covenant maker. Up until this point in scripture God is making promises, to Abram. In the first verse of the 15th Chapter of Genesis we gain a little insight into God's perspective. It reads, *"After those things the word of the Lord came unto Abram in a vision, saying, Fear not, Abram: I am thy shield, and thy exceeding great reward."* Think back to Genesis 12:2, when God says that He will make Abram a great nation, He would bless him, his name would be great, and he would be a blessing. God said He would bless Abram, but that blessing was separate form the blessings already listed.

Why is that significant? The question that came to me when I read it was, "If that's not his blessing, then what is?" In Genesis 15, we see a partial revelation. God tells Abram, He is his shield and his exceeding great reward. Reward in that scripture translates to the Hebrew word *sakar* which means, "*payment* of contract; concretely *salary, fare, maintenance*; by implication *compensation, benefit:* - hire, price, reward [-ed], wages, worth".

Did you see that? While we have a tendency to look for tangible things in the form of blessings, God told Abram, that *He* was his protection and the payment for the contract. What I found hilarious in reading this was Abram's immediate response to this revelation. He asks, "Lord GOD, what wilt thou give me…" That is funny yet remarkably sad, *but* God doesn't smite him for asking! God says, 'I am your reward' and Abram's response is that's great! But what are you going to give me?

It would be easy to get self-righteous, but the sad truth is we have all been guilty of wanting something other than what God has provided for us (I know, I stepped on my own toes). God says I will never leave you nor forsake you and we say 'Okay, that's great but what about this? Can you give me this?'

We saw Abram's question, now consider God's response found in Genesis 15:4:

"This shall not be thine heir; but he that shall come forth out of thine own bowels shall be thine heir. And he brought him forth abroad, and said, Look now toward heaven and the stars, if thou be able to number them: and said unto him, so shall they seed be".

This should encourage your soul! We can have moments of complete shortsightedness and because God is loving and merciful, He will spiritually draw us out of our environment and at the same time bring us closer to Him to remind us of the promise (note, the scripture said God brought Abram 'forth and abroad').

Spiritual Blind Spots

Have you ever been looking for something and someone was telling you where it is and you just couldn't seem to see it? That is what happens to us with God. He tells us what He has for us, but we can't seem to see it. We have to be like Abraham! We have to be able to spiritually see what God is showing us! We must learn to believe what God says.

Because Abram believed in the Lord it was counted to him for righteousness (Gen. 15:6, Gal. 3:6). This seems like a high point right! Abram believes and then God shifts the promise back to the land. God reminds Abram that, this was why he brought him out of the Ur! He led him out of what he was familiar with to give him an inheritance. Likewise, God led you out of whatever situation you were in, in order to give you an inheritance. What is interesting in this text is that God gave Abram the land but it still required him to work to get the people who already lived their off of it.

Believe in the Lord, Not in the Promise

Genesis 15:6 is the most important part of Abram's life. It reads, *"And he believed in the LORD; and he counted it to him for righteousness"*. When I initially saw this verse a number of things ran through my head. First, I initially paraphrased it and read it, "And he believed the Lord". However when I sat back down and re-read the scripture I saw that it actually says, "And he believed *in* the Lord".

Isn't it interesting how much of a difference one word makes. It wasn't that Abram didn't have faith. After all, he left when God made the initial promise in Genesis 12. However, I would like you to consider that perhaps Abram was so caught up in the promise that he never really believed in the Promiser.

You may be asking yourself how that can be possible. Let's say a radio station offers you money for if you are "caller number 10". You call not because you have confidence in the company, but simply because the offer was made. Abraham did that very thing. He was told if you leave I will do this for you, and he left. At this is point in scripture we find that Abram has shifted from believing in the promise to believing in the Promiser.

We have all been told to believe *in* the promises of God. I would suggest we are slightly wrong in our thinking. We should believe the promises of God, but believe in God. It is only when we believe in Him that our faith is in the right place, and we can be fully useable by Him.

What you will find in the remainder of the 15th Chapter of Genesis is God entering into a covenant with Abram. We serve a covenant God! Covenants can play out a couple ways. There can be responsibility on the part of both parties or only on one party. Abram asks God, "Lord God, whereby shall I know that I shall inherit it" (Gen. 15:7)?

Here is where the awesomeness of God shows up yet again! God doesn't get mad, but He breaks it down in a way that Abram could grasp the severity and gravity of His word. God told Abram to get some animals and prepare them so they can enter into a blood covenant.

Abram fell into a deep sleep and God began to tell him what would happen to his descendants. He tells him that they will be strangers in a land that is not theirs; they will serve them, and will be afflicted for 400 years (v.13). God will judge the nation they serve and his heirs will leave with more than they had when they went in (v.14). Abram will die in peace and at an old age (v. 15). And, after four generations they will return to the land they were promised (v. 16). This shows us that while God may have promised us something, because it is ultimately tied to His vision it will outlive us! It will pass for generations after us, and although it won't all be easy, every last word will come to pass.

Not everything in scripture rose to the level of blood covenant. They were reserved for important matters. It's like the difference between owing a friend some money, and you telling them you will pay them back. And, you trying to go to the bank and enter into a verbal agreement for the loan for a car! Because the loan is so important there is a more required to make sure you know what the consequences are for the agreement you are making, should you default.

Back then, it was customary for the participants in the blood covenant to walk between the halves of the animal carcasses to signify they would uphold their end in the covenant. If you did not uphold your end of the covenant you were held responsible and the consequences could be dire (See Jeremiah 34:18-22).

However, Abram did not pass through the carcasses. Only God did (Genesis 15:17)! The words of Hebrews 6:13-14 come to mind, "For when God made promise to Abraham, because he could swear by no greater, he sware by himself, Saying, surely blessing I will bless thee, and multiplying I will multiply thee". The act of entering the covenant was to show Abram, just how serious God was. God walked between the carcasses Himself, and took on complete responsibility for the promise. All Abram had to do was believe and walk it out without getting in the way.

CHAPTER 7

The Progression of the Promise

"Jesus Christ the same yesterday, and to day and forever".
Hebrews 13:8

We have a tendency to look at God like He is the one that keeps changing His mind. The word of God says that He is the same yesterday, today and forever more (God, Christ, and the Holy Spirit being one). We however, act like God changes His mind! Be assured of this one thing, if God promised it, it will come to pass…IF you align yourself with His will, have faith that He is able, and walk in faith and obedience. The promise that God gives us grows. It progresses and expands until the point of delivery. Let's take a look again at Abram and Sarai and the progression of the promise given to them and relate it to the promises God gives us.

Your Environment Matters

In Genesis 12, Abram was a 75 year old man. Pretty content I'm sure with life. He had been living for a minute after all. We learn a key element of the lives of Abram and Sarai in Genesis 11, Sarai was barren. It should be an encouragement to you, to know that something viewed as a dire situation is nothing but an opportunity for God to blow your mind.

The scripture reads, "But Sa'-rai was barren; she had no child". That, one word *but* at the beginning of the chapter says a lot. They were married, BUT she was barren. I take this to mean that they both wanted children but were aware that she was not physically (or spiritually if she knew it or not) able conceive a child.

In order for God to get her to the point that she was able to conceive, carry, and deliver a child she had to progress in her walk with Him, as did Abram. God decided to work His vision through a promise to Abram. The promise begins in Chapter 12 with the Lord telling Abram to leave everything he was familiar with and go. If he went, God said He would bless him. In the initial promise God is concerned with the environment Abram is in.

Did you know that in order to conceive in the natural the environment has to be optimal for conception? Remember the hostile womb? We are responsible for our internal environment, spiritual environment, but we cannot neglect the natural. There are some people and some things that we KNOW are not conducive with the things of God. Therefore we also know (if we want to acknowledge it or not) that our environment is not conducive with seeing the promise of God manifest in our lives.

Your environment is important because it helps to shape who you are. It is so important that Paul wrote plainly to the Corinthian church, 'Wherefore come out from among them, and be ye separate, saith the Lord, and touch not the unclean *thing;* and I will receive you,'(2 Corinthians 6:17) . Here we have Paul delivering a message to the church that applies as much today as it did then. Come out! In other words change your environment, *and* be separate. Separate translates to the Greek *aphorize* – meaning, 'to set off by boundary".

God is telling us come out from them and set some boundaries. Paul goes on to implore the church not to 'touch' which in the Greek is *haptomai,* meaning, *'to* attach oneself to' the unclean (or ungodly) things. What are you attaching yourself to? We cannot receive the promises if God, if we are attached to ungodliness.

Your environment exposes you to elements, which can either help or hurt you. While we may never know concretely what God was removing Abram from, let's be sure to view this from the proper perspective. There was something that Abram was associated with that would prohibit him from receiving the promise. But, because of his obedience to the Lord we will never know what issues, tests, and trials he bypassed. All we need to know is that he did.

Everyone Can't Go

We all say that everyone can't go with us. That everyone can't handle where God is taking us. So then, the question becomes why are we so determined to bring everyone with us? God told Abram to leave his family. Sometimes in order to get what God has for you, you have to not only be *willing* to walk away (willingness is always theoretical and does not necessarily translate to action). You have to walk away from some things and some people. Am I saying for you to arbitrarily write your family and friends off? Or course not!!! What I am saying is, if God says leave, even if it means leaving your family and friends you should leave.

You've Reached Your Destination

Genesis 12:7, "And the Lord appeared unto Abram, and said, Unto thy seed will I give this land". In this verse we see God expanding the scope of the promise. The promise has shifted and if you aren't paying attention you could have missed it. God announces to Abram in this verse that he will have seed, and that he had finally made it to the destination God desired for him to reach. God does not send us out wandering around with no indication of where we are going or if we have arrived.

Don't allow the enemy to lie to you by telling you that you are nowhere near your destination and that God isn't going to talk to you. He is a liar! But, if he can get you to believe that God just has you out there wandering around, then you may just turn around and head back to where you started.

Come Into Compliance

In Genesis 13, we see what happens when out of kindness, past relationship, or some sense of familial obligation we take people on the journey that were never really meant to be there. In Genesis 12, God told Abram to get away from his family. Abram got away from all but one, his nephew Lot. In the 13th Chapter of Genesis we see an altercation trying to arise between Abram's herdmen and Lot's. Abraham takes the initiative (perhaps realizing, he brought this on himself) and SEPERATES himself from his nephew, giving Lot land that he should have never had!

In the 15th verse God tells Abram, all the land that he can see He will give to him and his seed. Not only was the second expansion expanded upon, but he added more to the promise. In the 16th verse God tells Abram that his seed will be innumerable. Note that Abram wasn't included in the promise as a possessor of the land until he was fully compliant with the Word of the Lord. After he came into compliance (full obedience) he was also a recipient. Until then it was all going to his seed!

Are you being 100% compliant with the word the Lord gave you? If not you are being disobedient and disobedience has consequences. Are you like Abram and you are beginning to realize I didn't really cut all ties? I kept a few because, 'that's my girl' or 'that's my boy'. Have you kept relationships out of a sense of camaraderie? Are you attached to something that is 'ungodly'? If God told you to separate yourself and you didn't it's an ungodly attachment. If God told you never to attach yourself in the first place and you did anyway and haven't separated yourself, that is also an ungodly attachment.

If you are walking in disobedience you limit the work of God in your life. He is not going to reward disobedience. And you will only see a small portion of what God could have given you, if you even see that. Don't settle for less than He intends for you have. I would encourage you to think about the relationships in your life and if you know of some that God has explicitly told you to separate yourself from, please do! Don't write yourself out of your promise because of disobedience.

No Substitutes

There is a tendency for us to make our own solution to something that isn't even a problem. Abram looked at his situation in natural and saw that he was old and his wife was barren…that was a problem. God told him he would have an heir, but how? Solution: let's make my servant my heir! Now, I have someone to pass all of this too and God was right!

Here's the thing. There was no problem. He just didn't know nearly as much as he thought. But at least, Abram had the sense to ask God what He thought before making a move. We likewise must consider that not every idea we have is God's will for us.

The Lord essentially told Abram not to settle for a substitute! News flash anything other than what God has for us is a substitute for something much greater. We have all seen a knock off. It may look pretty good, but there is something about the quality that just isn't quite up to par. At the end of the day the original is always better than the substitute! Abram wanted to have his servant be his heir and the Lord told him that he would have his own son.

In Genesis 15, we witness the shift from promise to covenant as discussed in the last chapter. God shifts the responsibility to Himself and enters into the covenant with Himself concerning what He already promised Abram. God explains to Abram what will happen to His generations for literally hundreds of years to come. God doesn't just tell him the good stuff; he tells him the whole story. Why is this significant? We will not see everything that is attached to our promise. Prayerfully, your promise will outlive you, because we serve a God who reigns forever!

Also, Abram is given some sign about how he will live out the rest of his days. He would go to his fathers in peace! What a promise to have. I think if I were Abram I would have found comfort in knowing that. The Lord also let him know that he would be around for a while longer. God let him know that he would live to an old age. God goes on to tell Abram specifically where the land is. His land spans from the great river of Egypt, to the Euphrates.

There is to be no uncertainty with God. When we can handle the details of the promise God will give them to us.

A New Name and a New Covenant

From the beginning of the promise in the 12th Chapter of Genesis until the 17th Chapter 24 years have passed. 24 years!!! God starts the conversation telling Abram who He was. He announces himself as the Almighty God. God tells him that He is ready to make another covenant between He and Abram and that He would multiply him (v.2). The Lord tells Abram that he will be the father of many nations. He then changes his name! From Abram which means exalted father to Abraham which means father of a multitude!

What do you call yourself? Here is something to consider, whatever you call yourself should align itself with the vision and promise God has given you. There are some things that apply to all believers. If you are more than a conqueror than why call yourself defeated? If you are never alone, then why claim that you are abandoned? Be mindful of what you call yourself!

The first covenant God entered into with Abram didn't require for Abraham to do anything other than follow the instructions for preparation. However, this time Abraham would have to do something to symbolize to God that he and his heirs and all that worked for him were a party to the covenant. They had to be circumcised. This made it an everlasting covenant between God, Abraham, and the people. The covenant was that Canaan would be an everlasting possession and that God would be God not only to Abraham but likewise to his heirs.

Sarai wasn't left out of the name change either! Her name changed from Sarai which means dominative (fairly accurate description) to Sarah which means 'noble woman' (Brown Drivers Briggs). God says that He will also bless her, give Abraham a son from her, that she will be the mother of many nations, and that kings of people will come from her!

After Abraham laughed within his heart at the absurdity of all of it and has his moment of doubt reminding God that he and Sarah were old and asking about his first son Ishmael. God tells him that Sarah would have a son and his name will be Isaac and that he would establish his covenant with Isaac and his seed. Then God tells Abraham that Sarah would have Isaac in the next year.

We serve a God that is ready at all times to blow our minds! We have to realize that like with Abraham and Sarah there may come a time when God requires something of us and we should be more than willing to give it!

Keep Your Eyes Open

Although the promise started with Abraham, in order to come to fruition it was necessary that Sarah catch the vision and receive the promise of the Lord. We will now walk through this final phase of the promise before it actually manifests in the natural!

The 18th Chapter of Genesis starts with the words, *"And the Lord appeared unto him in the pains of Mamre: and he sat in the tent door in the heat of the day; and he lift up his eyes and looked, and lo, three men stood by him; and when he saw them, he ran to meet them and bowed himself toward the ground"* (verses 1-3). There are a couple things we're going to look at. 1) God doesn't always announce Himself and 2) it is up to you to be able to recognize Him with you see Him!

Abraham was in his tent sitting down. If you look at the scripture it says that Abraham saw three men and he recognizes one of them as the Lord! Would you be able to recognize God from a distance and then assume the right position? Abraham immediately let God know that he knew who He was.

What is your first reaction to the presence of God? Do you immediately run into a list of things you want Him to fix? Do you have a list of things you 'need' Him to do? Or do you recognize you are in the presence of the Creator of heaven and earth who owes you nothing and is worthy of your worship? Abraham was a worshipper! We saw in previous chapters that no matter was going on Abraham knew how to worship the Lord. We must get to that place. God doesn't need your worship, but he desires those who recognize who he is. Then and only then can you worship Him in spirit and in truth.

Abraham then asks the Lord to stay, so he can bless Him and the Lord does. Question…How often do you bless the Lord? It is in this time of hospitality that the Lord adds more detail to the promise. Sarah is cooking and the Lord asks where she is. Abraham tells Him and God says, "I will certainly return unto thee according to the time of life; and lo, Sarah thy wife shall have a son, And Sarah heard it in tent door which was behind him" (Genesis 18:10).

When Sarah hears this, her response is the same as her husband's! She laughs within herself! Here's the thing, she wasn't expecting the Lord to hear. The Lord asks Abraham why Sarah laughed and followed up with the question we all need to ask ourselves while we wait on His promise, "Is any thing too hard for the Lord?" (Genesis 18:14a). That is a question that we *should* all know the answer to. However, when faced with obstacles, trials, tests, and even the occasional "wait" we act like whatever we are waiting on, falls outside of the scope of God's deity! Strong statement, but it is the truth. Take comfort in the fact that despite what the enemy tells you there is NOTHING too hard for the Lord. The only one functioning on limitations is the enemy!

The Lord followed that question up with a reiteration of the promise, "At the appointed time I will return unto thee, according to the time of life, and Sarah shall have a son" (Genesis 18:14b). There is an appointed time for the promise to manifest! You can't rush it. When it is both your appointed time *and* your time of life the promise has to show up!

Abraham's promise progressed based on his walk with Christ, so did Sarah's. The same applies to you. God knows how much he can trust you with now, but rest assured as you increase in your intimacy with Him, He will reveal more to you.

CHAPTER 8

Delivering the Promise

"For the vision is yet for an appointed time, but at the end it shall speak, and not lie: though it tarry, wait for it; because it will surely come, it will not tarry".
Habakkuk 2:4

When you get to the final stages of pregnancy you experience worry, joy, impatience, excitement, and anxiety! It is the end of one season of your life, yet the beginning of another one. You experience the anticipation of seeing your child, along with the anxiety associated with the responsibility that must follow. This is also what happens spiritually.

When we are on the verge of seeing the promise of God manifest, this is also when we are most likely to want to stop the process. All of a sudden, it's real, not that you didn't know it was before, but in your mind, you had time to prepare. Experiencing labor means that you have passed through the season of preparation and now you are in the final stages before the promise manifests in the natural! However, before the promise is manifest there is one final step, delivery.

In the natural we know that labor is a painful experience, there can be measures taken to lessen the pain, but the pain is real. The same is true spiritually. You cannot expect to birth the greatness of God without being willing and able to bear and withstand the pressure and pain associated with its delivery.

Contractions

A spiritual contraction is the tightening of your spiritual muscles to enable you birth what God has given you. Take it from me, a mother of four boys, contractions *suck*, but without them surgery is required for birth (which coincidentally sucks more). Here is the question. You may be thinking, I've been pregnant forever, how will I know when I can deliver? It is not determined by you. When the promise has matured enough to be live, labor will begin.

Throughout the pregnancy, you have maintained a safe environment for the promise to thrive. There is a God ordained amount of time required for the promise to grow and develop enough to be able to live. Likewise there is an amount of time that you need to grow and mature to be able to protect and nurture the promise.

Contractions are a necessary part of the birthing process. Please bear in mind that the closer you get to deliver the promise the longer the contractions will be, you will have shorter recovery time between contractions, and the more intense the pain will become.

Spiritual Braxton-Hicks

In the natural women experience what is called Braxton-Hicks contractions. These contractions are considered by many to "practice" contractions. They are irregular and vary in intensity. However, they do not advance labor or delivery. Spiritual Braxton Hicks contractions are pains that do not advance your pregnancy but they prepare you for actual labor. Spiritual Braxton-Hicks much like regular Braxton-Hicks contractions in the natural can be stopped by a change in your position.

Spiritually, we need to move closer to God when we begin to experience contractions, it is the only way to know whether you are in true labor or if you are experiencing false labor. If it's time for the promise to manifest then moving closer to God will bring you comfort, but it will not stop the process.

However if you are in false labor, God knows it is not time for you to birth the promise. But the only way to stop the pain is for you to change your position and get closer the Father. This teaches you to turn to Him when you experience discomfort. He allows you to learn from the experience and take what you learn into the actual delivery, without causing premature delivery.

Premature Delivery

What the Lord promises us can be delivered prematurely. Premature delivery can result in an immature, underdeveloped, and malnourished promise. A promise that is not capable of surviving in the natural. The promise has to then enter a spiritual incubator so it can mature enough to survive!

Spiritually we prematurely birth things more often than we realize. You may be wondering how do I give birth to something prematurely and not know it's premature? A good indication that the promise is premature is if it requires constant attention.

In the natural premature babies are more at risk for disease and permanent disability. This mirrors what happens spiritually when there is a premature delivery of a promise. Spiritual immaturity can be fatal to the promise. It can be fatal because it has not matured enough. Babies that are delivered full term are small and vulnerable, yet resilient. However, they still require attentive care to ensure proper growth and development.

Premature babies often require periods of time in incubators to protect them from an environment they are not adequately mature enough to survive in. Spiritually when your promise is birthed prematurely; you will find yourself in a period of incubation. Please don't view it as punishment. It is a period of time that is divinely mandated to ensure that the promise does not die, and is not contaminated by the people or environment surrounding it.

When a promise is birthed prematurely there will be a lot of focus on ensuring its survival. However, Christ did not come for us to survive, but He came in order that we might live! If you find yourself always struggling to ensure the survival of the promise, I would suggest that perhaps the promise was delivered pre-maturely and as such, neither you nor the promise had the opportunity to fully mature to level necessary for spiritual life.

This does not have to be a fatal error. You can submit the promise to the Lord and allow Him to mature you, so that you can see and experience the fullness of life God intended. In other words, acknowledge that you moved prematurely and give it back to Him.

Promise Delivered

You have experienced the conception of the promise, maintained a safe environment to ensure its growth, development, and maturity. Your relationship with the Lord has deepened to levels that you previously didn't even know existed. You have dealt with the Braxton-Hicks contractions, and prevented pre-mature delivery. But wait this thing still hurts! You are in those final stages and all that is left for you to do is push!

There comes a point in natural child birth that you think to yourself, 'I just want this to be over! It hurts so bad!' Be encouraged the promise is on the way. Your job now is to push and breathe! Push your way past thoughts of quitting and failure. Push past the thoughts of your past mistakes and sin, push past the enemy and deliver what God has for you!

You will need a mid-wife, someone that can see what you are not in the position or state of mind to see. The mid-wife let's you know when you should push, when you should wait, and reminds you to breathe. It is someone who can encourage you, because they can see the promise, when all you can see is the pain.

You may not know where you are in the process, but after you deliver you get a sense of release and relief. Then you hear the baby cry and all the pain, complications, and time seem like nothing. God wants you to know that when you birth what He has promised you, it will make every tear, every pain, every doubt, and every fear seem like nothing. Because you can now see in the natural, what your faith was working so hard to protect.

It's not enough to simply deliver the promise! The condition of the promise is vital as well. Our goal as believers should be to deliver a mature promise capable of living and in turn producing fruit in our lives and in the lives of others.

As you continue this journey through life and recount the many promises that the Lord has made to you, remember that God has looked at you and found you worthy of a promise! The very least we can do as believers is ensure that not only we grow and mature in our relationship with Him, but that the promise matures and is made manifest in earth.

I would like to leave you with this thought. God's promise to you does not benefit anyone, not even His Kingdom if it never manifests! Remember the promises God has made to you, and make the decision to walk in faith, and obedience to fulfill your part in is His plan. You can deliver the promise; you *can* see it come to pass!

EPILOGUE

When the Promise Transforms
Bishop H.D. Ware Jr.

And, being assembled together with them, commanded them that they should not depart from Jerusalem, but wait for the promise of the Father, which, saith he, ye have heard of me.
Acts of the Apostles 1:4

Being that I am "product of the 1970s", one of my favorite movies of all time is "Star Wars". This sci-fi flick had it all: lasers, flying star ships, lasers guns, death rays, laser beams, light sabers ... did I mention lasers? This movie had it all. When it first premiered in my home town of Chicago, my parents allowed my sisters and me to go see this movie on a Saturday afternoon. I had been given the opportunity of a lifetime to go see "Star Wars" when it first hit the theaters. Oh, how my heart pounded and raced watching the *Millennium Falcon* speed through the galaxy fighting off Darth Vader and the evil forces of the Empire; sometimes even evading the Empire by making a leap into hyperspace! Wow! What a movie!

The Christmas "Star Wars" hit the screens was probably the most pivotal Christmas of my life. Why? It was during that fateful season that the *Millennium Falcon* was being created and released as toy; seemingly for one special little boy. Now, as far as little boys were concerned, the *Millennium Falcon* was the ultimate choice of toys on our Christmas list. To have the *Millennium Falcon* as a toy would have been the talk of the play ground. Having this toy in your possession automatically put you in the big leagues. On the play ground, the boy who owned this toy was a MAN to be feared – and I knew this. For this to happen, I had to have a popular boy visit my home and actually play with the toy, though. And for a popular boy to come over and visit my home to play with a toy I had, you guessed it, actually have that toy.

That Christmas season, I was a man on a mission. I put on my best behavior. I did everything my parents said, and even resisted the urge to act up in class. I had a goal in mind – asking for a Millennium Falcon without the stipulation of being told "only if you're a good, little boy". I knew I was a being a good, little boy! In my mind, I had to have that toy. Having the *Millennium Falcon* was of the utmost importance. Being the possessor of a *Millennium Falcon* would erase any stigma of being known as the scrawny kid, the non-athletic kid, the kid who was always picked last… sounds like I have some personal experience in this arena, doesn't it?

As December 25th began to approach that year, the days seemed to drag on and on. We were getting closer and closer to Christmas, but there was no sign of a *Millennium Falcon* under our Christmas tree. The

Christmas tree was up, the Christmas light were up, some gifts were already wrapped and under the tree, but not one big enough to be a *Millennium Falcon*. Now mind you, at this time in my young life, I'm beyond the "red coat guy and a chimney". I knew who was doing the gift wrapping and the purchasing; as I stated before, I was a man on a mission. I had a firm grasp of who put what under a Christmas tree. Hence, I knew I had to do more than act right. If I really wanted a *Millennium Falcon*, I was going to have to go to pull out "the big guns" and assure myself I was going to get what I was asking for this Christmas. I had to make sure my dad was going to deliver on his promise to get me a *Millennium Falcon*. So in the best way a little boy knew how, I fell on my knees (each night) and prayed to God that my parents would get me a *Millennium Falcon*.

That Christmas morning, I awoke before anyone else. My parents were still in bed, my sisters were still asleep; even the sun had not fully crested in the sky. The darkness of the morning only added to my anxiety over my Christmas gifts. Since I couldn't open my presents before everyone was awake, I decided to just sneak a peek at all the gift-wrapped boxes… you know, just inspect the sizes and dimensions of each box to see if my trepidation could be eased. Knowing the floors in our home always creaked whenever anyone walked across them, I decided to make as few steps as possible… you know, just being considerate of my still sleeping family. Alas, even though I tried not to disturb anyone, the floors in our home remained true to form. Thanks floors!

To make a long story, short, my dad did purchase me a *Millennium Falcon*, but he didn't gift wrap it. What? Oh, no bother. The paper would have just gotten in the way. But, he didn't put it under the tree. That little bit of information did disturb me, though. When I asked my dad why he purchased the *Millennium Falcon* but didn't put it under the tree, he informed me of something that had not occurred to me AT ALL while I was praying. He said "Son, your toy is in a hundred different pieces – it needs to be put together before you can even recognize that it's actually what you asked me for." At that moment, he and I poured all the little pieces out of the box onto the floor, and I watched him transform my *Millennium Falcon* just as it appeared in the theatre. When my dad was through assembling all the little pieces into the very thing I prayed about, he handed it to me and said "Son, I was never afraid of you opening up the box and getting the present early – but it would have broken my heart for you to see the picture on the outside of the box, and the inside of the box not be what the outside promised." He said "Herman, you would not have known what to do with all the little pieces. All you knew was that you wanted what you wanted." He said "Herman, I kept what I promised hidden because had you opened the box without me being present, you would have thought I gave you something other than what I promised. You would have thrown all the little pieces away before they transformed into what you hold in your hands today."

Beloved, the Bible says in Romans 12:2 – "And be not conformed to this world: but be ye transformed by the renewing of your mind, that ye may prove what is that good, and acceptable, and perfect, will of God." When I think back on that Christmas, and how I prayed for the promise of a *Millennium Falcon*, what rings true about this story for our everyday lives is that every time we pray for the Father to deliver on a promise, we must remember, that promise has to materialize for my use. When Hannah prayed for a son, I firmly believe no matter how Hannah may have wanted her son to remain a baby in her arms, her vow to God was that she'd give him back to Him. The promise delivered a son; the miracle came when what she prayed for grew up became instrumental in bring about the line of David. When Moses lead the Children of Israel out of Egypt, I'm sure they never imagined being hungry and thirsty. But when they prayed, not only did they receive manna from heaven, but the miracle was that manna kept on coming day after day. When Jesus and the 12 Disciples fed the 5,000 men in the Bible, the promise delivered dinner out of the fishes and loaves, but the miracle was that 12 baskets of fragments were taken up afterward. What are we saying here? According to the scriptures, when we allow our minds to be renewed, something must be transformed in like fashion. But what is being transformed? Beloved, we are being transformed – so that we can prove what the will of God is for our lives. Now what will this do? What this will do is make the hand of God evident in our lives by measure (the good, acceptable, and perfect). Remember, the Bible states in Romans 12:3 that every man has "the measure of faith." Put simply, this measure of faith has been given for the moment of transformation. This is because when the spiritual materializes in the physical realm, it is sometimes in hundreds of little pieces that only God can discern. This is why we have the measure of faith. We have the measure of faith because as soon as we pray for the promise, God starts to reveal what has already been in operation prior to us praying about our particular situation. Little by little, God reveals where He's been at work and what He's been doing on our behalf for our promise to transform. And when it transforms, it transforms into a miracle. Miracles are the proof of where the Word of God has been at work in the spirit realm, and is now beginning to manifest in the physical realm.

Beloved, realize we are required to be people of faith (Galatians 3:11). This faith allows us to not only create the perfect conditions to birth our promises, but when our promises are birthed, conditions are right and proper for them to transform into miracles. And remember, it is God who puts all the little pieces together in our lives to where all the good and the bad things which happen in our lives start to "work together" to transform into something God saw all along. Take heart beloved: let us not focus on all the things which try to distract us. God is going to give us it ALL to His Glory and to His Honor. Believe me when I tell you promises do transform into miracles.

APPENDIX

This book was birthed through an assignment I was given by my spiritual father, Bishop Russell L. Freeman. I was tasked with preaching a brief sermon on January 1, 2011. Out of that sermon, this book was birthed. My prayer is that it will bless your life, as much as it has blessed mine.

Be Blessed,

Elder T. Stevens

Sermon Transcript

"You Want It, But Can You Carry It?"
January 1, 2011
Elder T. Stevens

I have learned over my past thirty years of life that we live in a never ending cycle of seasons. We often preach about seasons and it use to irk me because nobody ever really talked about what it was. It was just your season or it wasn't. And I'm like dude , who are you, but that's just me. And so, very rarely do we get the opportunity to see the end of one season and the beginning of another season. Most of the time, we think that because our status changed or that because our situation has changed that our season has changed. They don't always work together like that, every once in a while your status can change and your season still be where you were before you got promoted.

So the Lord showed me that we just concretely got to see the ending of one season in the form of 2010 and we are now at the beginning of another season, but it imperative that before you go to make your resolutions, as to what you gonna do this year differently as compared to what you did last year, that you recognize that most of the time our resolutions don't concern God. They're things that we feel like we can do on our own. I'm a workout more, I'm a laugh more, I'm a work less, I wanna get promoted. And God said you never consulted me about any of that, and so you really right now think that you can do something by yourself, but you can't. And so, in the words He told me, 'the only thing you can do by yourself is go to hell'! That's it... And I was like well dang! And He was like you didn't come to me by yourself, my spirit quickened you to acknowledge that I AM, so you didn't even do that by yourself. I had to talk to you, to get you to realize that you were messed up, but here you go making plans for your life, without consulting me.

And so He said sometimes your plans for yourself, Toya's plan for my life do not always line up with what He has designed for me. And He said that He had spoken some things over everybody here in the past, and we want Him to do new things. When He has already spoken things that you don't see, but because you don't see it you want to write it off and you just want to move on to something different. Well He ain't do it, so God just give me something else. So He said, I want you to think about something that I promised you, that you don't see. Something that you know you can't for yourself. Something that you wrote off, cause I promised it so long ago, it just don't look like it'll happen. Now get that thing in your head, y'all thinking about it? I got mine. And my thought for today is "You Want It, but Can You Carry It?"

We often get caught up in the church in other people's birthing of things. And we see other people pregnant and it's like a virus, and so you're pregnant so I'm pregnant! They, they had a conference. Well... God called me to have a women's conference. And God said before you can get pregnant, you first have to conceive it. And I know y'all are thinking what is she talking about?! Conception is necessary before you can be pregnant. We have a tendency to get caught up n other people's stuff and put on 30 pounds of sympathy weight, and start, having sympathy pains, and complaining about your back hurt and everything smells funny and you're not even pregnant!

When God promises you something it is like you being pregnant. You change and you grow. And what He put in you is growing and it's developing. You change and you grow, and it's growing and it's developing. But before you even get to the pregnant stage you have to have a relationship with God. Not one born out of convenience or need, as in I need something therefore now God I need you, but tomorrow when I don't need it I'm good and I'll talk to you next time I need something. That's convenient and that's not a relationship! And you wouldn't deal with anybody who only called you when they needed something. You would be like, do you have anything to offer me or is it always about you? Always!

So turn to Hebrews Chapter 11, the eighth verse. When you get there say Amen. I'm not gonna read without ya'll so y'all are gonna have to let me know when you get there. It reads:

Heb 11:8 By faith Abraham, when he was called to go out into a place which he should after receive for an inheritance, obeyed; and he went out, not knowing whither he went.

Heb 11:9 By faith he sojourned in the land of promise, as *in* a strange country, dwelling in tabernacles with Isaac and Jacob, the heirs with him of the same promise:

Heb 11:10 For he looked for a city which hath foundations, whose builder and maker *is* God.

Heb 11:11 Through faith also Sara herself received strength to conceive seed, and was delivered of a child when she was past age, because she judged him faithful who had promised.

Through faith also, Sarah herself received strength to conceive seed. Through faith, also Sarah herself, we aren't talking about Abraham's faith right now, cause Abraham didn't have the problem. Sarah had the problem. Through faith also Sarah received strength to conceive seed. Not mess, not gossip, not back bighting but a seed, a seed that was promised to her by God. And was delivered of a child, we have people that are professional pregnant people, they don't ever birth anything. She got pregnant and she birthed it, because she had faith. You're just professional pregnant people, you don't ever birth nothing. You always waddling, your back always hurt, and you don't ever birth anything. She through faith received the strength, the strength *dunamis* is what strength goes back to, that power that ability. She lacked the ability and the capacity to birth or hold anything, she did not have a foundation and because she didn't have a foundation God didn't trust her with anything. Because when you develop a relationship you are developing trust. That's why she judged him faithful, because *He* promised. And she began to think about everything else He had already promised that he already brought to pass. But it was a process, it was a process.

She was the person that had the fertility issue. She announced in Genesis 16, that God has closed my womb. So she knew she couldn't have any kids, and she knew why she couldn't have any kids, but she still wanted kids. But instead of consulting God on the matter, she decided hey, in her own words, "it may be", it *may* be. Not it's gonna be. Now we're gonna function off of the possibility of somebody else's actions. Because she thought she had control over her maid. Because the maid is supposed to do what the master tells them to do right?!?! So, it may be that I may obtain children by her. But when Ishmael was born, she didn't have that child. That was his other wife's child! He only had one wife in the beginning, but now he has two because she had a bright idea, and didn't want to consult God on the matter, first.

I don't even think that she was helping God, because if you read the text there is no indication that she knew what God had promised to Abraham. Which is why husbands and wives should have conversations and major in communication, because now I'm going off something that I don't know God already told you, you were gonna have. And so if you 'gon have then I'm gon' have it and there's no need for me to make it myself. But because she made it herself she had to deal with the consequences of it. For 14 years I have to watch my husband, and this chick, ad their kid! And I don't like to share, so I'm sure she don't like to share either, and ya'll don't like to share either!

So what the Lord said to me was, when I promise you something and you don't see it come to pass, the question becomes what is it LaToya on the inside of you, that is so nasty that it will contaminate what I put in you. I was like, is it like that? And he said is your womb at best hostile or are you barren? And I was in the bed about to go to sleep when He said that, and I was like I have a hostile womb Jesus? What is a hostile womb you know? He's like let's start with being barren where getting pregnant just is not an option. It don't matter what you do, you're not gonna get pregnant. You can go to the doctor, and spend all your money. You can come up to the prayer line and Bishop can lay hands on you, you can fall out and you *still* won't get pregnant, because God said I closed it. I closed it. Or as he told me is the problem with most of the people in church, is your womb hostile?

And a hostile womb is one in which your womb creates an environment that kills the deposit that was put on the inside of you before conception can ever occur. Or by chance you conceive it, so you got the vision, God gave you the vision, you conceive but the environment in your womb is still hostile and aborts it on its own. Ain't nothing wrong with it, it's you. Your body says I don't know that, it's foreign, kill it. Your immune system turns on what God deposited in you, because it doesn't recognize it. So God says I developed a relationship with you and I trust you, and now I put it in you, and you don't trust *me*? You don't trust me. That's what it boils down to, is trust.

She did not have a foundation and because she did not, God closed her womb. Her lack of a foundation is what kept her sterile. And it was not until she moved beyond that, I'm gonna get done on my own. I'm a make it happen, cause that's what I do I make stuff happen. That God said ok, no, no, no, no, no, she don't get it. Let's let her walk that out for a little bit. Until she figures it out that because *I* said that's why it will be. Not because of what you can do, but because I said it.

So when you fast forward in the account of things you get to the 18th Chapter of Genesis. When Abraham is at his tent I'm paraphrasing' y'all, but read it, it's a good read. And he's minding his business sitting at the door of his tent and he sees three people walk past and he runs to them to meet them and then he recognizes that one of them is the Lord. And God said to me you have to understand that when I promise you something, it's then your responsibility to look for me, because I'm not always going to announce myself to you. Sometimes I'm on my way to go handle some business, and if you want something from me you, then you need to be able to recognize me when you see me.

So he saw Him and was like let me bless you, let me cook you something to eat, get you some water, because that's why you came by. And it was at that point that the angels says do as you have said. And he asked him where was Sarah? Now up until this point God had not said a word to Sarah about a child. He's promised all of this to Abraham. And over time because Abraham had to develop his own relationship The promise that God made changed from being simply an inheritance, it got more detailed, It didn't change, it got detailed to you're gonna have an heir, then it move from your gonna have a heir to you're gonna have a son. Then it moved from you're gonna have a son, to you're gonna have a son with your wife, to you're gonna have a son with your wife in the next year. That was the progression of his relationship. 'Cause God knew what he could trust him with in the 12th Chapter of Genesis, when he was 75. He knew that when he got to be 100 he would be able to handle it. He also knew that Sarah was gonna cut a fool was he was about 88 and that she was gonna have to walk some things out until she was about 90.

So, simply having a vision doesn't make you pregnant. The vision is your direction to tell you how to go, and where to go and how to get there. But it is not the moment of conception. And, we confuse the two, because I can have a vision of being a millionaire and spend my whole paycheck and not save anything, and not tithe anything, and not offer anything, and still have the vision of being a millionaire and be 72,000 thousands in debt. Just because I have a vision does not make it so. That's a hope. Your vision is hope for the future, your faith makes it a now thing. Faith pulls from the future into right now. It was something that God promised me here, for some time out there so it's hope. But through faith, I say I have a child now, and I have a child because He promised. And we have to recognize, that when God promises us things there are usually conditions. Unless it's a prophecy like Jesus is gonna come.. Jesus was gonna come and it didn't have anything to do with what I did. But when God promises you something it is contingent upon your belief. Do you believe? If you don't believe you can pack up your crayons and go home. Cause it don't matter, the conversation is like null and void, if you don't believe. Not because God's not capable, but because you don't believe that He's capable and He don't have to prove himself to you.

So if you believe and your actions line up with your beliefs then you conceive. And then it's your responsibility to make sure carry it in an environment that is not hostile, so that it does not die for no reason. Because sometimes God does not give us stuff because He will not allow you to abort it. He said before I let you kill me MY vision, cause we think that it's our vision, you just won't get it. Before I let you kill MY vision. We like to co-sign with God. Anything that happens in the body of Christ is His vision. And He uses people to implement His vision. And that's why we can't follow folk, cause like Bishop said you don't realize it's not their vision anyway. So you can't submit, 'cause I think it's about who I like, and you can't see the forest for trees, and you ain't trustin' nothing. You ain't doing anything.

Sarah in time received the power of God to conceive what He promised to her, but she only got it when God saw that she was able to have it and not kill it. When He knows that we are capable of carrying and delivering what He has promised us with then He will give it to us. But it's only when you recognize, that it is because He promised it. I can promise to make you some cookies, and I make some pretty good cookies. But if life happens, and my kids get sick, or I get caught up in work and I can't get up here and bring the cookies, it don't mean that I didn't make them I just couldn't bring them. But, that's me and I'm human and I have things that I have work around and other things I have to account for. I have to account for my children, and my husband does he have something going on? Is someone gonna end up doing something and I can't go. But God is not like that. If He said He's gonna give it you, then He's gon' give it to you. But we treat Him like He's people, like He's good people but He's people.

And we say that we trust him, but we don't and we say that we can carry it, but if we could there would be more things being birthed in the Kingdom of God, than are currently being birthed. It's the same people giving birth and the same people watching them give birth, when *you* should be pregnant by now! And you say it's always the same people, it's always the same people at the church, always the same people with the Bishop. They always go with him when he goes. Well, where are you at? Where's your relationship with God? Are you pregnant? He's *(Bishop Freeman)* is like a midwife. He helps you deliver what God gave you, He can't make you pregnant. He can help you not to stress out, when you start stressin' out, so your blood pressure don't get high. But he can't get you pregnant and he can't make you have a baby. You need your own relationship with God for that.

And even though she was old and a lot of us say I'm too old for this, and I've been doing this for too long, or he promised it so long ago. She hemmed Him up by the laws of nature and time. And God told her at the appointed time at the time of life, I will return to you and you will have a son. So there is an appointed time, and there is a time of life. It is not always your time of life it is not always my turn. Sometimes it's someone else's turn, and sometimes I have to support them when it's their turn. Because if anyone is ever gonna support you, you have to learn how to support other people.

In Habakkuk 2:3-4 it reads, For the vision *is* yet for an appointed time, but at the end (at the end of the process) it shall speak which translates back to *puach*, which means breathe. And when babies are born everyone is waiting for what? That first breath! So, God said, at the end of the process at the end of your pregnancy, it will speak, and it will not be a lie. And although it's take a little longer than you would like for it to take, wait for it 'cause it's not a waste of your time. Our problem is we think we are wasting our time waiting on the things that God has promised. So we just come up with new lists, but I would encourage you to know what has God promised me that I do not see, and what do I need to do on the inside of me to see it come to pass? The person who promised it He is faithful and I have judge him faithful. And the Word of God says to basically be careful what you judge people by because you'll be judged by it too. If I'm judging God to be faithful, then I'm expecting Him to judge me faithful too when I'm looking at Him. And He can say she walked it out. It may have taken a little bit longer than she would have liked, but I knew how long it was going to take when I promised it to her in the first place. So your time line is not God's timeline.

About the Author

Elder LaToya Stevens was born in Colorado and currently lives in Missouri. She is supported fully in ministry by her husband Elder David Stevens. Elders David and LaToya Stevens are the proud parents of four sons: David, Marcus, Matthew, and Nathaniel.

In 2008, LaToya was licensed minister and was ordained the following year, in 2009 at Shekinah Tabernacle Ministries under the leadership of Bishop Willie J. and Pastor Margaret A. Curry. She is a prolific teacher and preacher of the Gospel, with a heart to see God's people live with the fullness and abundance of life that only He can give. She currently attends United Community Cathedral, where she is under the spiritual leadership and covering of Bishop Dr. Russell L. Freeman.

Other books by CECO Publishing:

In Breaking the Cycle: Mental Bondage Pastor Nikesha Luther teaches the important role vision plays in staying free of mental bondage and living the life of purpose God has for you.

To purchase please visit: www.cecofellowship.org/Store.html

www.ingramcontent.com/pod-product-compliance
Lightning Source LLC
LaVergne TN
LVHW041634070426
835507LV00008B/605